CITY SANDWICH

CITY
SAND

GREENWILLOW BOOKS
A Division of
William Morrow & Company, Inc.
New York

WICH

POEMS BY
FRANK ASCH

Printed in the United States of America

First Edition

10 9 8 7 6 5 4 3 2 1

Library of Congress Cataloging
in Publication Data
Asch, Frank. City sandwich.
Summary: Twenty poems describing
different aspects of city life from
a child's point of view.
1. City and town life—Juvenile
poetry. [1. City and town life—Poetry.
2. American poetry] I. Title
PZ8.3.A7Ci   811'.5'4   77-18902   (gr. 1-4)
ISBN 0-688-80156-0
ISBN 0-688-84156-2 lib. bdg.

To Janani

CONTENTS

Sunrise   11
The Best Street   12
Alley Cat School   15
The Sugar Lady   17
City Bicycle   18
Taxi   21
The Traffic Cop   22
Subway   25
Noise   27
The Zoo   29
A Wedding in the Park   30
Apple War   33
Fireman   35
Ballooning   37
Department Store   39
Laundromat   40
Fame and Fortune   42
Rooftop   45
Sunset   47
A City Pet   48

CITY SANDWICH

SUNRISE

The city YAWNS
And rubs its eyes,
Like baking bread
Begins to rise.

THE BEST STREET

In the early early morning,
When the city is almost quiet,
You can go out and hear the streets speak.
No kidding! Just try it.
"I'm the best street,"
        You'll hear the highway say,
"I get them where they want to go."
"I'm the best street,"
        says Broadway,
"I really give them a show."
"I'm the best street,"
        says Market Street,
"It's here that money changes hands."
"I'm the best street,"
        says Main Street,
"It's I who have the marching bands."
"I'm the best street,"
        you can even hear the alley say,
"To me come all the homeless cats and dogs
        that stray."

ALLEY CAT SCHOOL

Do alley cats go
        to alley cat school?
Where they learn how to slink
        and stay out of sight?
Where they learn how to find
        warm and comfortable places,
On a cold wintry night?
Do they learn from teachers and books,
        how to topple a garbage can lid?
Did they all go
        to alley cat school?
Is that what they did?

THE SUGAR LADY

There is an old lady who lives down the hall,
Wrinkled and gray and toothless and small.
At seven already she's up,
Going from door to door with a cup.
"Do you have any sugar?" she asks,
Although she's got more than you.
"Do you have any sugar," she asks,
Hoping you'll talk for a minute or two.

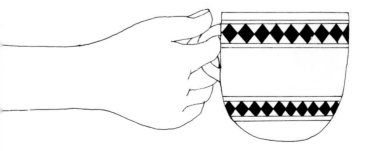

CITY BICYCLE

Clutching the handlebars
    Of my bike
Like the horns of a bull,
    Spokes flashing
        Feet pumping,
Dodging pedestrian matadors,
    With shopping-bag capes,
        From the sidewalk
            To the street,
I jet from the curb.

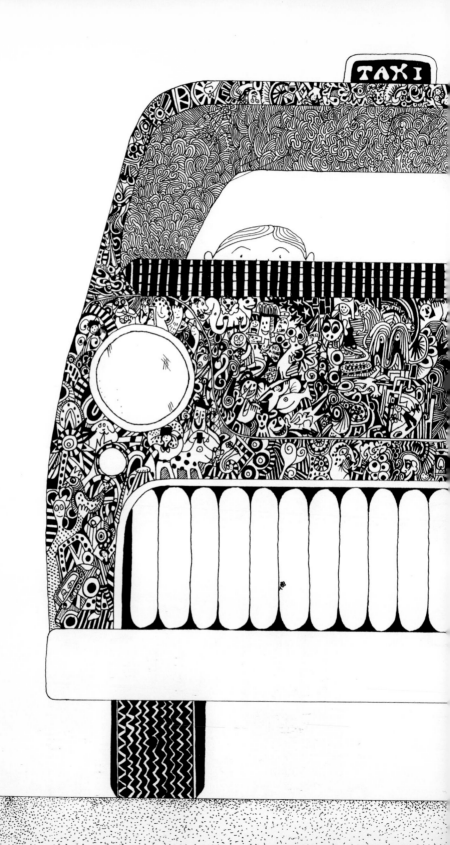

TAXI

Taxi! Taxi!
Step on the gas
Where to?
And make it fast
Step on the brake
Just in time
Faster faster
Left at the light
Down to the corner
Make the next right
Stuck behind trucks
Squeezed by a bus
Zig zag
Not so fast
Slow down
Pull over there
Taxi! Taxi!
What's the fare?

THE TRAFFIC COP

Garbage truck
    and bus
        and car,
Motor cycle
    and moving van,
      all
    STOP!
        for one man:
The traffic cop.

SUBWAY

I buy my token and wait
     for a while,
By the broken tile.
It's dark and damp and dreary
Until the train comes down the track.
With a swish and a roar.
     and a clickety-clack,
With
    CHICO
      KING
        CRAZYMAN
           5
Scribbled up and down its side.
(The subway always gives you more
     than just a ride.)

NOISE

Rat a tat tat
went the jackhammer
rrrrrrrrrrrrrrrrrr
went the plane
screeeeeeeeeeeeech
went the tires on the street
and drove me insane.
From then on when I heard
a fire engine clang
I pointed my finger
and shot it
                BANG! BANG!

When the next door neighbor sang
I shot him too
                BANG! BANG!

When the traffic roared
or the pipes hissed
I never missed.
And I was quick on the draw
when the telephone rang
                BANG! BANG!
                BANG! BANG!

THE ZOO

Everyone tries
To get the lions
     to roar
But they roar
When they want to
And not before.

A WEDDING IN THE PARK

One day in the park,
Where it was cool and shady,
The balloon man married
The flower lady.
When the soda pop man
Gave away the bride,
The chestnut man and
The pinwheel lady cried.
She gave him a flower,
He gave her a balloon,
And they floated away
On their honeymoon.

APPLE WAR

One, two, three, four,
They marched like soldiers past my door,
One, two, three, four,
They marched into the grocery store,
One, two, three, four,
They spent a dollar, not a cent more.
One, two, three, four,
They bought apples rotten to the core,
One, two, three, four,
They marched out of the grocery store,
One, two, three, four,
They marched like soldiers past my door,
One, two, three, four,
They had a rotten apple war.

FIREMAN

In his black hat
He drives a red truck
Through a red light
On his way to fight
The red and yellow flames.

BALLOONING

I like to sit on the fire escape,
  blowing up balloons,
And tossing them down into the street,
Watching where they go,
  and what they do.

Some hurl their bodies,
  before oncoming buses,
Some bounce along the sidewalk,
  pretending to be businessmen,
Some are captured by children,
  and taken home.

One, I remember, was chased by a dog,
Until it slipped down
  an open manhole.
The dog sniffed and went away,
But the balloon reappeared.
Hitching a ride on the wind,
  up it flew,
One hundred stories high,
  and down again.

DEPARTMENT STORE

Teacups and toys,
And rocking chairs,
It's got a bird that can sing,
Grandfather clocks,
And flower pots—
It's got a little of everything.
Going to the big department store—
It's the kind of store
That makes me smile—
I'm not going to buy anything,
Just going to visit awhile.

LAUNDROMAT

With checks and plaids
    and polkadots,
With stripes, corduroy,
    and terry cloth,
With underwear and towels,
     with dungarees and shirts,
That foam and slosh and spin,
    around
        and around
           and around,
The laundromat is a dizzy world.
With checks and plaids
    and polkadots,
With stripes, corduroy,
    and terry cloth,
With underwear and towels,
     with dungarees and shirts,
That foam and slosh and spin,
    around
        and around
           and around.

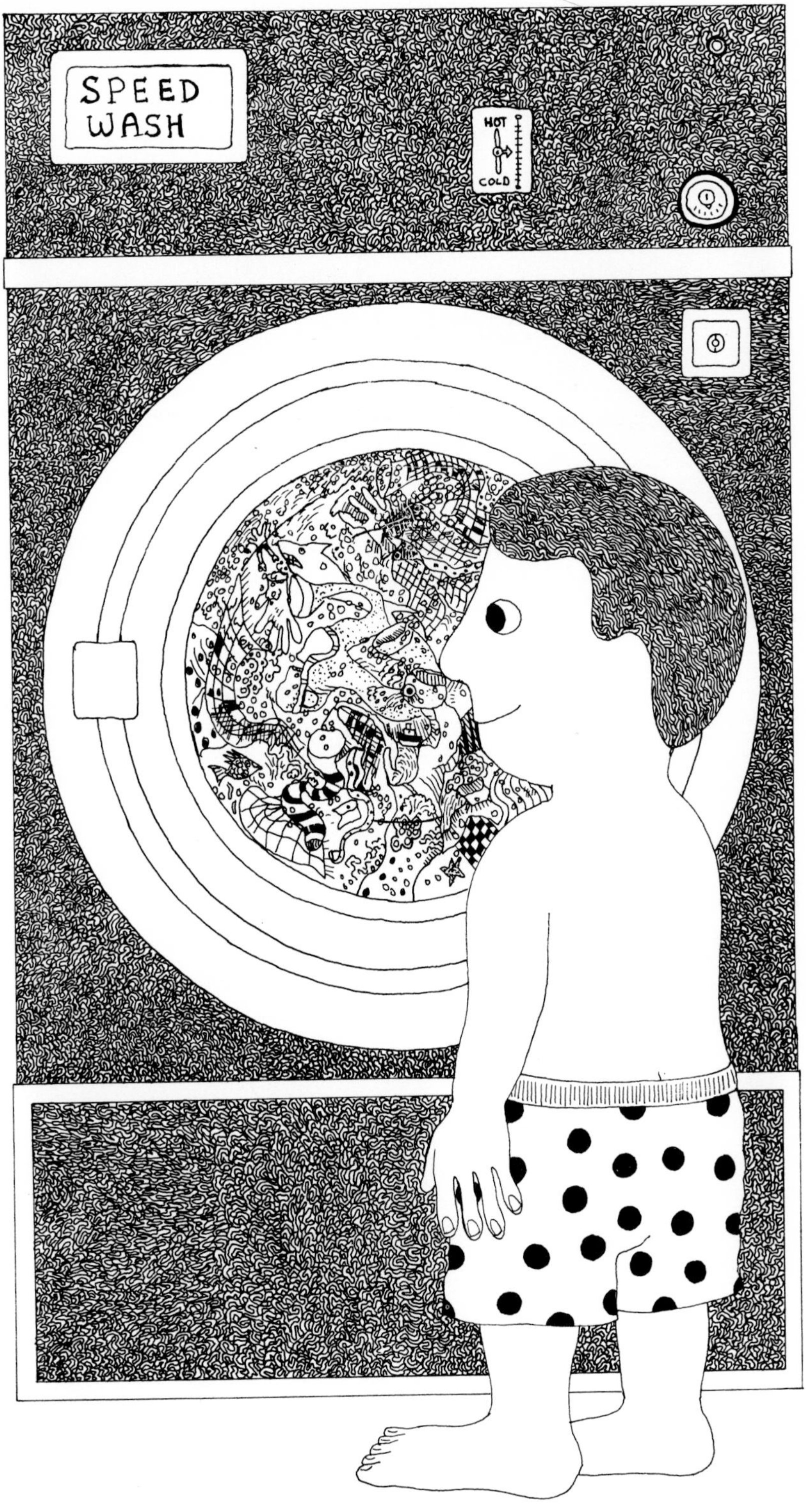
SPEED
WASH
HOT
COLD

FAME AND FORTUNE

Fame: Through the doors
       past the garbage
        in the hall
    Up three flights
       somebody wrote
        MY NAME
    on the wall.

Fortune: We lowered
      the bubblegum
        through the sidewalk grate
    Pulling nickels and dimes up
       steady
       and
       straight.

ROOFTOP

Street sounds
of backyards
and playgrounds
make a symphony
  that never stops.
And the best seats
are up on the roof,
where the music
curls gently
  round the chimney tops.

SUNSET

The sun goes down.
Its glow ignites
The city sky
With neon lights.

A CITY PET

Goldfish by the window,
Swimming in the moonglow,
If I lived in the jungle,
You'd be an elephant.

Goldfish by the window,
Swimming in the moonglow,
If I lived in the country,
You'd be a horse.

Goldfish by the window,
Swimming in the moonglow,
Maybe when we move to a bigger place,
You'll be a dog.